First Questions and Answers about Dinosaurs

Did Triceratops Have Polka Dots?

TIME
LIFE *for*
Children ®

ALEXANDRIA, VIRGINIA

Contents

What is a dinosaur?

Dinosaurs were the ancestors of today's birds, but they didn't have feathers and they couldn't fly. Dinosaurs lived millions of years ago. We think of them as huge, but some were smaller than you are.

The word "dinosaur" means "terrible lizard." The people who first found dinosaur bones thought the bones came from terrible dragons or giant lizards. Scientists now think dinosaurs were more like birds because their skeletons are alike and they probably behaved the same way. Like most birds, dinosaurs built nests, laid eggs, and cared for their babies.

5

Why aren't dinosaurs at the zoo?

The last dinosaur died a long time ago. That's why living dinosaurs are not in zoos or forests or any other place on Earth. When a certain kind of animal dies out and is never seen again, we say it is extinct. Dinosaurs became extinct long before the first people lived, so no one has ever seen a living dinosaur.

6

DINOSAUR
MUSEUM

Did you know?

The dinosaurs died 65 million years ago, but the relatives of some animals that lived then can be seen today. These include turtles, sharks, crocodiles, and cockroaches.

How do we know about dinosaurs?

We know about dinosaurs from fossils. Fossils are a special kind of rock. They keep the shape of plants and animals that lived and died long ago. People have found fossils of dinosaur bones and dinosaur teeth buried in the ground. They have also discovered dinosaur eggs, and even dinosaur footprints!

Fossils can tell us many things about a dinosaur. If the dinosaur's teeth were sharp and pointy, it probably ate meat. If its teeth were flat, it probably chewed plants.

9

Who named the dinosaurs?

The first person to write about a new dinosaur fossil gets to name the animal. A dinosaur's long name is written in the languages of Latin or Greek. Its name often tells you something about the dinosaur. Many dinosaurs are named for the way they must have looked. Others are named after people or places.

Stegosaurus means "covered lizard." It was named for the bony plates on its back.

Lambeosaurus means "Lambe's lizard." It was named after dinosaur scientist Lawrence Lambe.

What was the world like when dinosaurs lived?

Dinosaurs wandered through forests, deserts, rivers, and lakes that were very much like the ones you see today. Even some of the animals were the same. The dinosaurs lived with frogs, lizards, and insects such as dragonflies and cockroaches. There were a few big differences, though. There wasn't any grass, and the North Pole was so warm that it had no ice. Can you imagine that?

Hey! How about a ride?

Did you know?
Dinosaurs lived on Earth a very long time. The ones in this book lived at different times—and in different places, too.

13

Could dinosaurs fly?

No, but other animals could. They were called pterosaurs. Some pterosaurs were as small as pigeons. Others were much bigger. Pteranodon had a body the size of a turkey, but its wings were very long. If Pteranodon lived today, its unfolded wings would stretch from the front of a school bus all the way to the back! Pterosaur wings were made of thin flaps of skin. The animals were very good at gliding.

Did you know?
The biggest pterosaur, Quetzalcoatlus, measured almost 39 feet from the tip of one wing to the other. It was the size of a small airplane!

Did dinosaurs live in the water?

No, dinosaurs stayed on land. Other animals, including giant crocodiles and turtles, lived on land and in water. Still other creatures stayed in the water all the time.

Ichthyosaurus resembled a giant porpoise. Look at all those sharp, pointy teeth!

Elasmosaurus looked like a sea serpent. Its neck was as long as its body.

Deinosuchus, a large crocodile, laid its eggs on land but spent the rest of its time in the water.

Which dinosaur was the biggest?

One family of dinosaurs, the sauropods, came in three sizes: big, bigger, and supercolossal! One of the largest sauropods was Seismosaurus, whose name means "earth-shaker lizard." Seismosaurus was longer than a blue whale. Unlike people, dinosaurs kept on growing until the day they died.

Which was the smallest?

That would have to be Compsognathus. This little dinosaur was less than 30 inches long and weighed only 15 pounds. That made it about the size of a chicken! Some other small dinosaurs were named Saltopus and Heterodontosaurus.

Heterodontosaurus

Compsognathus

Did you know?
The smallest dinosaur fossils ever found were baby dinosaurs still inside their eggs. They were only two and a half inches long. That's smaller than a crayon!

Saltopus

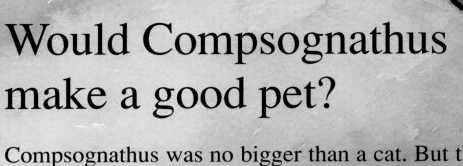

Would Compsognathus make a good pet?

Compsognathus was no bigger than a cat. But that doesn't mean it would make a good pet. This little dinosaur was a hunter with pointy teeth and sharp claws. It ate lizards, frogs, and other small animals. So even though Compsognathus might have fit in your lap, it was too fierce to make a safe pet.

23

What did dinosaurs eat?

Dinosaurs ate the same sorts of things that are eaten by animals living today. Most dinosaurs ate plants. But others were meat eaters that hunted for their food. They ate many animals—including other dinosaurs!

Allosaurus hunted other dinosaurs. It had 60 sharp teeth.

Brachiosaurus was tall enough to nibble leaves from the tops of trees.

Don't worry! I'm a vegetarian!

Baryonyx may have used its claws to catch fish for its meals.

25

Which dinosaur was smartest?

Some dinosaurs hunted in packs. They needed to be smart in order to work together. One of the smartest of these hunters was Troodon. This meat-eating dinosaur was not very large, but it had a big brain for its size. Troodon's brain was about the size of a tangerine.

It's smart to work together!

How did dinosaurs protect themselves?

Meat eaters could make the dinosaur world a dangerous place, but plant eaters had many ways of staying safe.

Stegosaurus had pointy spikes on its tail. During a fight, it swung its tail as a weapon.

Take that, you prehistoric punks!

29

Did you know?
Other dinosaurs could run and hide.
The color of their skin may have helped
them blend into the land around them.

Size helped protect
sauropods like
Diplodocus. Who
wants to fight some-
thing that big?

Ankylosaurus had
bony plates all over its back
and sides. Like a turtle's shell, the
plates protected it from sharp teeth and claws.

How fast could dinosaurs run?

One of the fastest dinosaurs was Hypsilophodon. This little plant eater was about the size of a large dog. It had strong back legs and a small body. Scientists think Hypsilophodon could run about 25 miles an hour—that means it could keep up with a car going down your street! It had to be quick, because meat eaters like Velociraptors could run fast, too.

Did you know?
The biggest dinosaurs were also the slowest. Giants like Seismosaurus moved only as fast as a person walking.

31

Did Triceratops have polka dots?

No one knows for certain what color the dinosaurs were. Fossils can show the shape of things long ago, but they can't show their color. Dinosaurs may have been green or brown, like many snakes and lizards. It's also possible that their skin had patterns to keep them hidden. This means some dinosaurs may have had spots like a leopard, or even stripes like a tiger!

BODY PAINTING TODAY!

Did you know?

Scientists believe that some dinosaurs had bright, colorful patches that helped them attract a mate.

Why did Stegosaurus have a bumpy back?

Those big bony plates probably kept the animals from getting too hot or too cold. When the sun shone on the plates, it made the animal feel warmer. When the wind blew past the plates, it took away heat and cooled off the dinosaur. Imagine that—an air-conditioned dinosaur!

Did you know?

The plates also could have helped males and females attract each other. Or they might have been used to scare off other dinosaurs.

How big was a baby dinosaur?

Compared with their mom and dad, baby dinosaurs were pretty tiny. They had to be small, because they hatched from eggs. If an egg gets too big, its thin shell will crack. Since dinosaur eggs couldn't be too big, neither could the babies inside.

Maiasaura parents were much bigger than elephants, but their eggs were only the size of grapefruits. When the babies hatched, they were just two feet long.

How did dinosaurs take care of their babies?

Most dinosaurs built nests to hold their eggs and took care of the babies after they hatched. Maiasaura built nests near one another so they could watch and protect the eggs together. When the baby Maiasaura hatched, their parents brought them food. Later on, the parents showed the young dinosaurs how to find food for themselves.

Did you know?
"Maiasaura" means "good-mother lizard."

39

Did dinosaurs travel together?

Some dinosaurs, including Maiasaura and Triceratops, traveled in large herds, looking for food. Giant sauropods like Apatosaurus also lived together, but in much smaller groups. They kept their young inside a herd of grownups, where meat-eating dinosaurs could not get to them. Small meat eaters such as Deinonychus hunted together in a pack, like wolves, so they could catch larger animals.

Did you know?
Not all dinosaurs stayed in large groups. A big scavenger like Tyrannosaurus roamed around by itself, looking for dead animals to eat.

41

Could dinosaurs talk?

Dinosaurs could not talk the way people do. But they may have been able to squeak, chirp, honk, or howl! One dinosaur that probably made a lot of noise was Parasaurolophus. It had a hollow, bony crest on the top of its head. When air went through the crest, it might have made a honking or tooting noise. This might have attracted another Parasaurolophus, or it may have warned other dinosaurs that trouble was near.

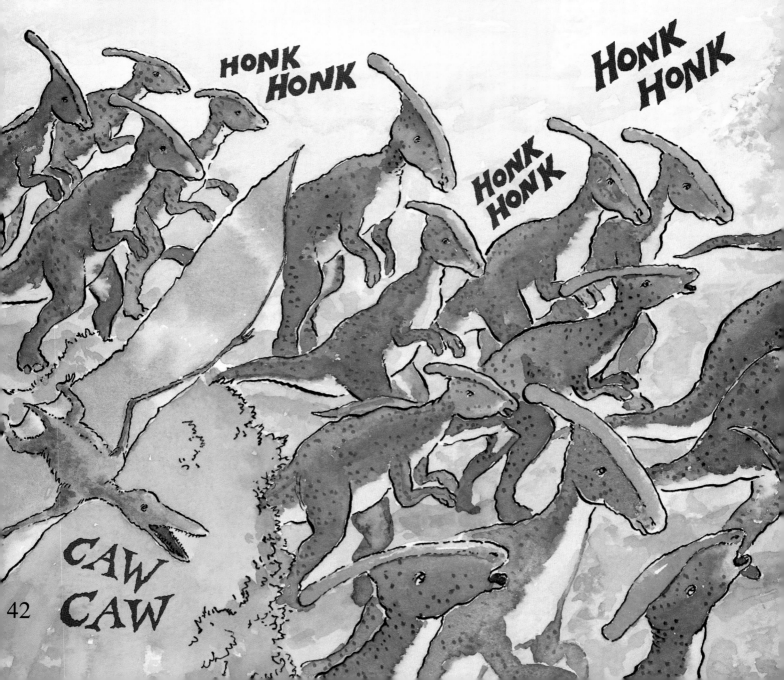

43

Why did the dinosaurs become extinct?

Scientists are not sure, but they have lots of ideas about why the dinosaurs died out. They think something must have happened a long time ago that changed the world in ways that were not good for dinosaurs. A big stone from space may have hit our planet, raising dust that blocked the sun and made the weather too cold for the dinosaurs to live. So, after millions and millions of years of life on Earth, the dinosaurs disappeared.

Did you know?

Scientists think that some dinosaurs did not really die out. Instead, they may have changed into other animals over a very long time. So when you look at birds, you may be seeing the relatives of dinosaurs that lived long ago.

45

Why do we like dinosaurs so much?

People of all ages are fascinated by dinosaurs. They remind some people of dragons and other make-believe creatures from fairy tales. If you like scary monsters, it's fun to think about dinosaurs. One of these incredible creatures might even have lived on the land where you are right now!

TIME-LIFE for CHILDREN®

Managing Editor: Patricia Daniels
Editorial Directors: Jean Burke Crawford, Allan Fallow,
Sara Mark
Senior Art Director: Susan K. White
Publishing Associate: Marike van der Veen
Editorial Assistant: Mary Saxton
Production Manager: Marlene Zack
Senior Copyeditor: Colette Stockum
Quality Assurance Manager: Miriam Newton
Library: Louise D. Forstall, Anne Heising

Special Contributor: Barbara Klein
Writer: Andrew Gutelle

Designed by: David Bennett Books

Series design: David Bennett
Book design: David Bennett
Art direction: David Bennett
Illustrated by: Peter Kavanagh and Jim Kavanagh
Additional cover
 illustrations by: Nick Baxter

First printing. Printed in U.S.A.
Published simultaneously in Canada.

Time Life Inc. is a wholly owned subsidary of THE TIME INC. BOOK COMPANY.

TIME-LIFE is a trademark of Time Warner Inc. U.S.A.
For subscription information, call 1-800-621-7026.

School and library distribution by Time-Life Education, P.O. Box 85026, Richmond, VA 23285-5026

Library of Congress Cataloging-in-Publication Data

Did triceratops have polka dots? : first questions and answers about dinosaurs.
p. cm.—(Time-Life library of first questions and answers)
Summary: Questions and answers provide a wide variety of information about dinosaur characteristics and behavior.
ISBN 0-7835-0903-0 (hardcover)
1. Dinosaurs—Miscellanea—Juvenile literature. [1. Dinosaurs. 2. Questions and answers.]
I. Time-Life for Children (Firm) II. Series: Library of first questions and answers.
QE862.D5D465 1995   95-18649

567.9'1—dc20   CIP
                                                                        AC

Consultants

John R. Horner is curator of paleontology at the Museum of the Rockies and adjunct professor of biology at Montana State University in Bozeman, Montana. Among many other books and articles, he has authored *Digging Dinosaurs: The Search That Unraveled the Mystery of Baby Dinosaurs* and the children's book *Maia: A Dinosaur Grows Up*. He was awarded an honorary Doctorate of Science by the University of Montana in 1986.

Dr. Lewis P. Lipsitt, an internationally recognized specialist on childhood development, has received the Nicholas Hobbs Award for science in the service of children. He has served as the science director for the American Psychological Association and is a professor of psychology and medical science at Brown University.

Dr. Judith A. Schickedanz, an authority on the education of preschool children, is an associate professor of early childhood education at the Boston University School of Education, where she also directs the Early Childhood Learning Laboratory. Her published work includes *More Than the ABCs: Early Stages of Reading and Writing* as well as several textbooks and many scholarly papers.

How to Say Those Big Words

Allosaurus: AL-uh-SORE-us

Ankylosaurus: ang-KY-lo-SORE-us

Apatosaurus: ah-PAT-o-SORE-us

Arkansaurus: AR-kan-SORE-us

Baryonyx: BAR-ee-ON-icks

Brachiosaurus: BRAK-ee-uh-SORE-us

Compsognathus: komp-sog-NATH-us

Deinonychus: dye-NON-i-kus

Deinosuchus: dye-no-SOOCH-us

Diplodocus: di-PLOD-uh-kus

Elasmosaurus: ee-LAZ-moe-SORE-us

Heterodontosaurus: HET-er-oh-DON-tuh-SORE-us

Hypsilophodon: HIP-sih-LO-fuh-don

Ichthyosaurus: ICK-thee-uh-SORE-us

Lambeosaurus: LAM-bee-uh-SORE-us

Maiasaura: MY-ah-SORE-uh

Parasaurolophus: PAR-uh-SORE-uh-LOAF-us

Pteranodon: te-RAN-uh-don

Pterosaur: TEAR-uh-sore

Quetzalcoatlus: ket-sahl-co-AT-lus

Saltopus: SALT-uh-puss

Sauropod: SORE-uh-pod

Seismosaurus: SIZE-muh-SORE-us

Stegosaurus: STEG-uh-SORE-us

Triceratops: try-SER-uh-tops

Troodon: TRUE-uh-don

Tyrannosaurus: tie-RAN-uh-SORE-us

Velociraptor: ve-LOSS-i-rap-ter

Time-Travel to the Land of the DINOSAURS!
DINOSAUR MUSEUM
Opens Today!